C000091105

ISBN: 9798403315876

Cover design by: Art Painter
Library of Congress Control Number: 2018675309
Printed in the United States of America

CONTENTS

LEARN TO SEW BASICS

How to make

BUNTING

The perfect introduction to learning how to sew.

By Sarah Foster

INTRODUCTION:

You want to learn how to sew! Fabulous. Without a doubt, making a pretty line of bunting is most definitely a good place to start.

The great thing about having this guide is that you can really take your time, there is no need to remember everything you saw in a video and you can refer back to it as and when you need to. I've also included some handy pictures as we go along.

In this step by step guide, I will take you through the fun process to making some beautiful, high quality and professional looking bunting with some tips and ideas to help make your bunting stand out from the rest. Before long you will be producing lines of it and your family and friends will be wanting you to make it for them too.

Let's get started!

TOOLS:

What you need: Get prepared before you start! I believe that preparation is key to just about everything in life, even for sewing a line of bunting. If you plan ahead and organise before you start, the whole process will be much easier and so much more enjoyable, so please do read the following rather than diving straight into the 'fabric cutting' section!

These are my tools for making bunting:

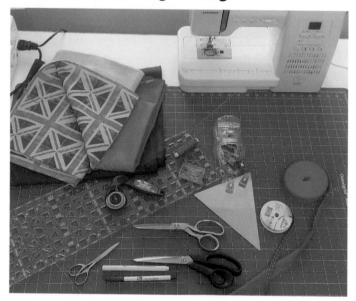

Scissors. 'Obviously', you may say! But, here's the thing; you can't use just any old scissors that have been knocking around in the kitchen draw for years! You need a good pair of sharp fabric scissors. These are available from many haberdasheries, craft stores and online at really affordable prices. Buy the best you can afford, good scissors are an investment for any sewer. Ideally, get them from a shop where you can go and handle them to make sure that they feel comfortable in your hand. Check the weight and length of them, it's probably best not to go for a pair of tailor's shears just yet! I'd suggest a cutting length of around 10cm to 12.5cm (in old money that's about 4 to 5 inches). You can see the scissors I will be using in the picture.

Roller Cutter, Quilting Ruler and a Self-healing Cutting Mat: These items are certainly not essential but if you are taking this sewing lark seriously and planning on making a lot of bunting or perhaps thinking once you've mastered bunting, you'll move on to a bit of patchwork, then this is a great investment and will reduce your cutting time drastically. I wouldn't be without mine but I do sew an awful lot!

Template: I think I mentioned I sew a lot and bunting is something that I just love to make for my online shop, so I had a special metal template made just slightly bigger than the finished size I like my flags to be, this then takes into account the seam allowance. You could measure out each flag on your fabric, I just find the template quicker. I would suggest that you make a template out of sturdy card to start with, which is how I started out. More about sizes will follow later.

Fabric Marker or Chalk Pen (or just a pencil for now!): For me the best way to mark fabric is with a fabric marker pen. They are great as the line disappears when pressed with the warm iron. To get you going, you could just use a biro or pencil, which I have done in the past. The only thing with a biro on fabric is that this can bleed into the material or you get ink on your fingers and then mess up the pretty fabric (yes! I've done that too – hence why I love my fabric pens). I use a purple one on light coloured fabric and the white one on dark coloured fabric.

Pins &/or clips: I've taken to using sewing clips lately for lots of projects, they are like miniature pegs and are a bit easier to handle than pins. I have less holes in my fingers when using this ingenious invention and they come in a selection of pretty colours too! Clips are especially good when you have several layers of fabric, as pushing a pin through can be tricky but, of course, you can still use pins & in some instances only a pin will do.

Sewing thread (& a couple of sharp sewing needles if you are going to be hand sewing): Pick a thread that is going to tone with the majority of your fabric colours. You don't have to match every flag with a coloured thread (but you can if you want to). The flags we will be making will be hemmed on the inside, so stitches won't be seen. They will be seen on the bias tape/ribbon though so go for thread that blends with that.

Sewing Machine: I don't envy you if you plan on hand sewing a huge long row of bunting but I have done it in the early days and when you get to the end it really is a satisfying achievement. I use a Janome sewing machine. Every sewer will have their preferred machine make, this just happens to be mine. It is easy to thread and creates several types of stitches and has an easy to understand instruction manual. My very first sewing machine, however, was incredibly basic with forward and reverse straight stitch only. A basic machine would be fine for creating oodles of bunting. Make sure you have a sharp point needle (not a ball point) as you will be sewing through layers.

Iron and Ironing Board: the only time I love to iron is when I am sewing! It's an essential piece of kit though, particularly for pressing out the bunting flags. Keep your fingers out of the way of the hot plate though!

Fabric: Woohoo! The juicy bit you've been wanting me to talk about! Picking out your favourite fabrics & deciding on colours is such fun. I'm like a child in a sweet shop when I'm picking out fabric. Alternatively, you could make some 'memory bunting' using your children's old clothes, old blankets, old shirts/blouses and you can reminisce as you make your bunting. Do clear it beforehand though with the owner of the clothes you are about to chop up! Aim for lightweight fabric like poly cotton or cotton. Avoid silky fabric as this is tricky to sew as it shifts and moves when cutting & sewing. Also avoid other stretchy fabric like jersey/T-shirt fabric for the same reasons of silk.

Bias Tape or Ribbon: I use 2.5cm/1" wide cotton bias tape when I am making bunting and a little bit of narrow ribbon for the loop ends. I buy my bias tape on 50m rolls. The rolls come in a vast selection of colours and are really easy to work with. If you want to use ribbon, I would recommend a cotton ribbon rather than a silky ribbon as silk ribbon is a little trickier to sew with, especially for a beginner, as it tends to move and slip around. You'll also need some narrow ribbon for the loop ends.

A Few Basic Sewing Terms:

I've tried to make this booklet easy to follow without using too much terminology. The following sewing terms are the first you learn when you begin sewing and they may crop up, so I have popped them here for you to refer to.

Seam allowance – this is the extra bit of fabric between the stitches and the edge of the fabric.

Raw edge – the cut edge of the fabric

Bias tape – this is a strip of fabric that has been cut 'on the bias' to give a stretchy tape for use in making all kinds of crafts and clothing.

On the bias – this is when you cut out pieces of your fabric diagonally along the grain of the fabric – it makes the fabric a bit stretchy and is used in making clothing.

The grain – fabric has a grain, it is how the fabric is woven together. It is more obvious in loosely woven fabric. The thread is woven up and down and side to side to create the grain.

Rights sides together – this is when you place two pieces of fabric together with the pattern facing inwards

Wrong side – the back of the fabric that isn't on show

Tacking (tack) – loose hand stitches that hold the pieces of fabric together so that pins can be removed before sewing in a machine.

FLAG TEMPLATE:

Decide how large you want your finished flag to be. My finished flags are approximately 16.5cm high by 15cm wide, so the size of my template is roughly 18.5cm high by 16.5cm wide. The template includes a 0.7cm (7mm) seam allowance all the way around.

Using a thick piece of card, like doubled up cereal box card, draw out the flag shape the size you want the finished flag to be (diagram 1).

Now mark 0.7cm (7mm) out along the straight edges and draw another line all the way around (diagram 2) – this extra space is called your seam allowance. You can make this bit bigger if you are hand sewing and make sure you do the same size all the way around and remember what you made your seam allowance for when you start sewing! For machine sewing 0.7cm is fine.

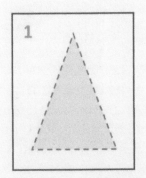 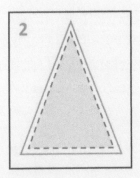

Carefully cut out the card triangle, cutting around the outer edge (as in diagram 2) to create your flag template – keep the card nice and flat. If you are using doubled up card I would make sure you glue the card together before cutting and then tape around the outside edges being careful to not ruckle the tape as you want a nice smooth edge. Template done! Ready for fabric.

FABRIC CHOICE & CUTTING

New fabric: If you are using new shop bought fabric, like me, still give it a little press before starting to make sure any folds are nice and flat and that there are no creases that will mess up your flag shape. If you want to use a patterned fabric featuring pictures or words, I recommend you opt for a fabric that has a random pattern where there is no direction for the pattern (ie: words & images go in all directions). Fabric which has say animals or words on it that all face in one direction will be wasteful when cutting out your triangles, unless you don't mind the pattern being upside down on some of the flags! I like to use poly-cotton and cotton. Avoid stretchy/silky fabric.

Old clothes: for example; an old shirt, cut the shirt to make a flat piece of fabric and press.

Backing fabric: I like to use a plain poly-cotton backing fabric to go with my patterned facing fabric, especially when the bunting is going to be hung against a wall.

Find the grain of the fabric, you want to have the grain going up and down and not diagonally. Cutting diagonally on fabric is called 'cutting on the bias' and this will make even your cotton fabric a bit stretchy. Look closely at the fabric and you will see the weave.

Level the bottom of the fabric: When you buy new fabric, the haberdasher may not have cut the fabric with a solid straight line, sometimes they don't cut but tear the fabric, so we need to have a nice straight edge to work from. Draw a straight line across the bottom of your fabric using a ruler/straight edge, taking into account the pattern if there is one and the weave. Cut along this line to make your straight edge, this is the edge that you will be working from.

Double thickness: To cut two flags at a time, fold the fabric in half (right sides together) making sure your triangle fits. If you have a pattern direction, you may need to cut the fabric in two & rotate one piece so that when you lay the fabric right sides together the pattern is going the same way on both, otherwise you will end up with the pattern being upside down on one flag. If in doubt, cut in single layers. You can also cut single layers of fabric if your piece of fabric isn't large enough to cut double thickness.

Place the short edge of the triangle template on the straight edge you have cut, either on the far left or far right hand side of the fabric.

Draw around the template. Once you have drawn around the template, lift off and move the template along, butting up the bottom corner of the short edge of the template to the bottom corner of the triangle you have just drawn on the fabric. Make sure the fabric doesn't ruckle up and keep the bottom of the template nice and level with the edge of the fabric. Draw around the template again. Continue working all the way along until you reach the other side of the fabric.

Hold on! Put those scissors down, we're almost there, we just have one more line to draw!

Draw a straight line using your ruler/straight edge all the way across the top points of the triangles you have just drawn. You've just doubled the number of flags you have drawn and created the next straight line to work from!

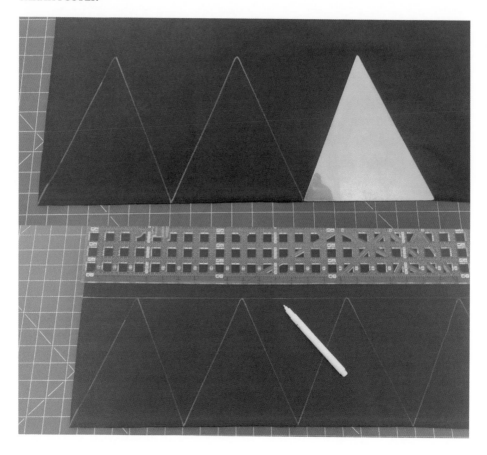

Now you have a choice: **1)** keep drawing triangles or **2)** start cutting. I choose to start cutting! If you are cutting double fabric thickness, pop a few pins in the fabric or clips to the edges to hold the fabric together ready for cutting.

Cut along the long straight edge at the top of the triangles using your scissors or rotary cutter. I tend to use scissors for this bit, especially if my fabric is wide as I just find it easier to handle. It's a personal thing!

Cut along the diagonally drawn lines this is where I go for the rotary cutter with the straight edge and cutting mat but scissor away if tha's what you prefer. Cut out all the triangles ready for sewing.

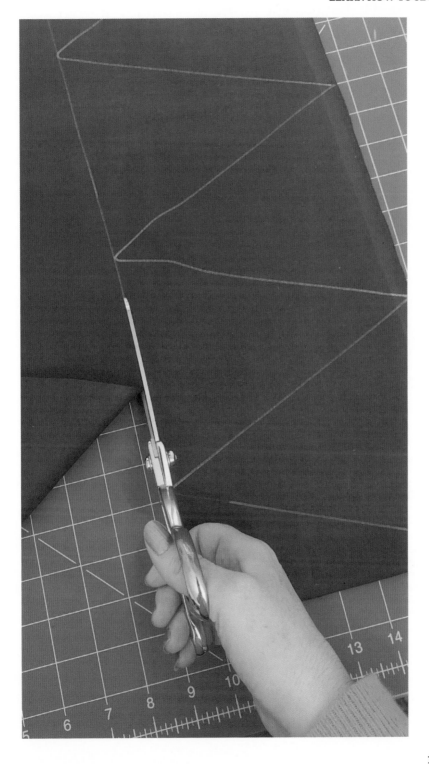

Repeat the above process until you have enough flags to make your string of bunting – don't forget, you need two fabric triangles for each flag, the front and the back pieces. I am going to make a string of 15 flags, this is the most popular size I sell in my online shop. On the front I'm going alternative pattern, then plain, pattern, then plain etc ending on a pattern. Therefore, I need a total of 30 fabric triangles. I'm using 8 in patterned facing fabric and 7 in plain fabric, plus 15 plain for the backing fabric making up my 30 triangles.

Below: the blue plain triangles on the left and the patterned ones on the right.

SEWING

With right sides together, pin or clip the backing triangles to the patterned (front) triangles. Remember, if like me you are using a plain backing fabric, you want one plain piece and one patterned piece. Right sides together simply means the pattern is on the inside. We will be turning the flags the right way out after sewing. You will now have 15 flags ready to sew.

Ready? Then let's start sewing!

Follow your sewing machine instructions for threading the machine. Take one of the doubled up flags and slip the top corner of the long edge under the presser foot with the short edge away from you (short edge at the back of the machine). Eye up where the needle will drop into the fabric and remembering to allow the 0.5cm seam allowance. Gently lower the presser foot down onto the fabric, keeping the edge of the fabric straight on to you.

Tip: If you look on your machine, there will be a ruler/sewing guide with numbers and you line the edge of the fabric up with the guide line. On my machine, I use the presser foot as the guide and place my fabric so that the edge of the fabric lines up with the edge of the presser foot & this is roughly 0.7cm.

Above: Flag in the machine, ready to start sewing.

Work slowly to start, remove the pins as you sew before they get to the needle to avoid damaging the needle. You can pick up speed when you are a bit more practised and confident. Use a straight stitch to sew & STOP a little before you get to the point of the triangle flag. Do not sew all the way off the fabric.

When you stop sewing near the point, make sure the needle is down into the fabric. Lift the presser foot up and rotate the fabric so that the second long edge is in line straight in front of you, drop the presser foot back down and sew all the way to the end & off the fabric. With the needle in the up position, raise the presser foot and remove the flag from the machine, snip the thread to detach. Sew the remaining 14 flags in the same way.

Above: Flag in machine turned and ready to sew the other side. See how I line up the edge of the foot with the fabric.

Turning the flags: You now should have all of your flags ready for turning. Before you turn your flags the right way out, you need to 'clip' the pointy bit close to but not into the stitches at the bottom of the flag, as in the picture below – this makes less bulk when turning the flags out – be very careful not to snip the stitches! Turn the flags the right way round and push the point out with a dull pencil or chunky round tipped knitting needle (make sure not to poke a hole all the way through).

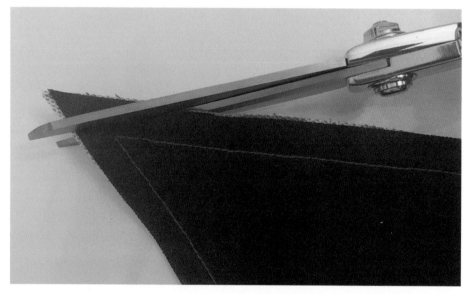

Above: snipping the tip ready for turning out the flag. Snip from both sides.

Iron the flags: Please don't skip this step! Do be careful when ironing the flags, your fingers will be close to the hot plate. If you are young or not yet allowed to use the iron, get an adult to help you here. Make sure to push the stiches outwards to keep all your flags the same.

With the flags all pressed out, you will see there are a couple of little ears at the top opening of each flag. Snip these bits off to give you a straight edge.

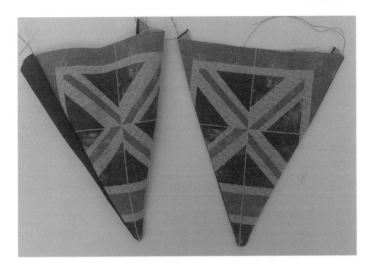

Above: see the difference pressing the flags with the iron makes. The left flag is turned but not pressed the right flag is pressed. See the little 'ears' that need to be snipped off too.

Adding the bias tape/ribbon: You'll need a nice flat & smooth, clean work top area to work on. I'm using bias tape from a roll. Because I don't need the bias tape to be too stretchy, I pull it from the roll and stretch it a little first in my hands and fold it in half, pressing between my fingers as I work along it. I won't cut it off the roll until I have attached all of my flags, that way it won't be too long or too short.

I measure about 25cm from the end of the bias tape and slide the unsewn (raw) edge of the triangle into the fold and then clip or pin that in place. When using pins here, be careful, as you are going to be pinning through several layers of fabric. Next, decide on what gap you would like between each flag, I tend to allow 8cm as I like to see lots of flags rather than lots of gaps. Slide into the bias the next flag and clip/pin, continuing all the way to the end, remember to allow another 25cm after the last flag is inserted, like you did at the beginning and cut the bias tape.

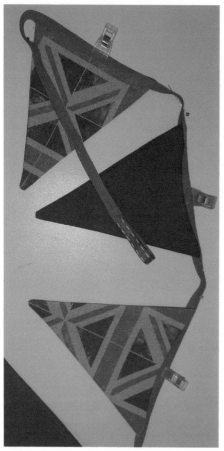

Loop ends: cut two short pieces of ribbon, I've gone for 15cm long. You want the ribbon to be narrow enough to slide into the folded bias tape at each end. Fold the ribbon in half to make a loop and slide the cut ends into each end of the bias tape so that approximately 2.5cm is inserted and clip/pin to hold in place. You can tack the ribbon loops and flags in place and fully remove all your clips/pins if you prefer but it isn't necessary. You are ready to sew the flags to the tape now.

We want to be sewing as close to the open edge of the bias tape as possible, ideally, keep the flags pointing to the outside (left) of the machine. Carefully, place the bias tape and ribbon loop end into the sewing machine, hold the ribbon/bias in place with your finger & remove the clip/pin, gently lower the presser foot onto the tape to hold in place, try not to trap your finger under the presser foot!

Sew the ribbon in place going forwards and back a few times to secure. I usually sew diagonally over the area where the loop is to ensure it is strong. Sew closely along the edge of the tape, removing clips/pins as you go and checking the flags are still neatly tucked into the bias tape. It's tempting to crank the speed up but I strongly suggest you take it slowly. When you get to the other end, remember to do the same with the ribbon loop to ensure it is strongly secured in place.

Pictured here: the loop end ribbon in the machine. Make sure this is good and secure!

Above: sewing the flags to the bias tape. Keep your stitches really close to the edge.

Another quick trip to the iron to give a final press and hey presto! You have made your first string of bunting.

Well done. Onto the next string! I've popped a few pictures of my finished line of bunting following.

I hope that you found this process easy to follow and most importantly that you have had fun and you will continue to keep sewing. Thanks. Sarah xx

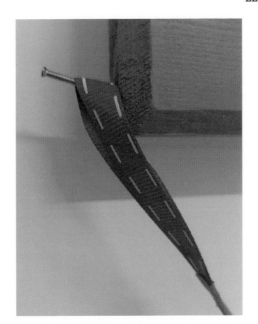

My bunting hanging in my sewing room. Just couldnt quite fit it all in to the picture! The total length of this bunting ends up just over 3m long.

Congratulations on making your bunting! Keep on sewing, this is just the beginning.

Bunting makes a fantastic gift, looks great in many rooms of the house, summer-houses and perfect on a sunny day in the garden. What would a garden party be without a string of dancing bunting, fluttering in the breeze.

Holidays are great for bunting too, I've made black and orange bunting with spooky fabrics for Halloween and Christmas bunting using festive fabrics to hang on the stairs. When you get established at making the bunting you can add appliques to the flags like cute chicks and colourful eggs for Easter time or lettering for a special event. Have fun with it. Happy sewing!

For more inspiration you can see some of my latest creations on my sewing website:

www.country-stitches.co.uk

Thank you for buying this booklet. I hope that you have enjoyed following the step by step instructions and you are inspired to create lots of bunting that will look great for many years to come.

If you have enjoyed this book, you may like some of my other books. Please visit my website for all my current works: **www.sarah-foster.co.uk**

Printed in Great Britain
by Amazon